A Glimpse of Yesterday

Saleta Gray

Presentation by *BookLeaf Publishing*

Web: www.bookleafpub.com

E-mail: info@bookleafpub.com

ISBN: 9789357740883

First edition 2023

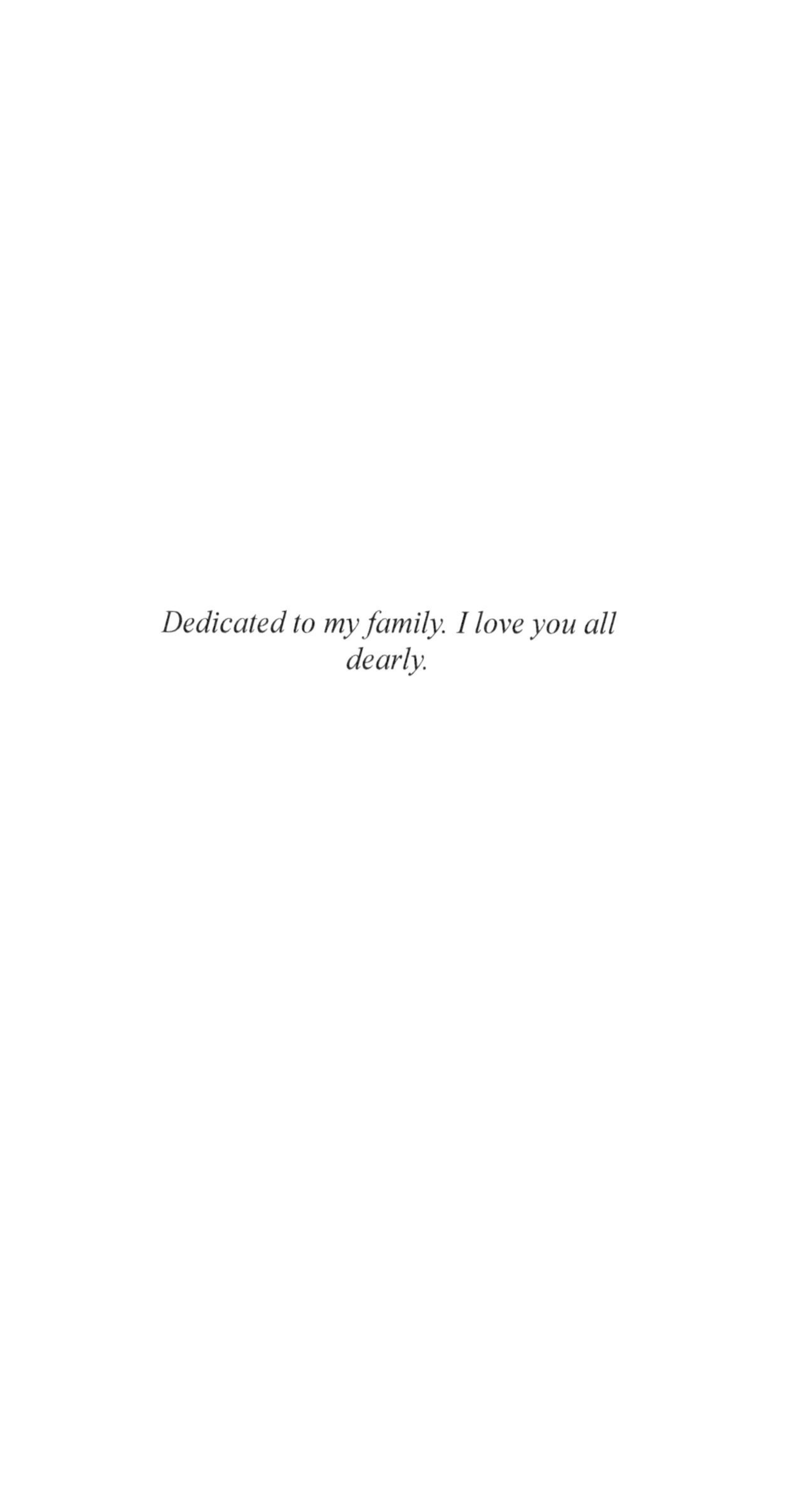

Dedicated to my family. I love you all dearly.

ACKNOWLEDGEMENT

Special thanks to my sister for always believing in me. Emilie, I love you so very much.

PREFACE

Every day of life offers something different...this is where inspiration lives. This is a glimpse into a day in the life of Saleta Anne Gray, one moment at a time.

Just Thinking…

Just Thinking…

I thought of you today, but that's nothing new. I think of you often, what else can I do. Just sit and think since you're not here, I'll shed a few tears and wish you were near. I'll think of the times we shared and the years you were here. I'll listen to the songs that remind me of you and go back in my mind to happier times before you were gone. I'll hang on to those memories until we meet again and always remember you were my very best friend.
<3 always, Saleta
Saleta Anne Gray

Pictures

Pictures

As I sit and look through photographs of us, I'm suddenly reminded of a moment of love. Never knowing if it will be the last, but definitely here to show me the past. Forever grateful for each memory captured, to serve as a reminder of a life that truly mattered.

Each one taken at different times, but linked together through space and time. Strangers who met through God's grand design, questioning nothing at this moment in time. The day we met was truly a gift, now saying goodbye is a more difficult rift.

The time we shared will forever remain, for pictures were taken again and again.

Saleta Anne Gray

17 Years

17 Years

17 years have come and gone,
And still your arms feel like home.
I never knew a love so true,
Until the day that I met you.
Side by side through thick and thin,
A love like ours will never end.
Until the day the Lord calls my name, with you
is where I will remain.
Loving arms to hold me tight, I thank God for
you every night.
I love you more today than the day we wed, I'm
looking forward to the next 17+ years.
All my love, Saleta
Saleta Anne Gray

It's Fall Y'all

It's Fall Y'all

The leaves are changing one by one, alerting us
that fall has begun.
Turning colors from green to red, reminding us
that cooler days are ahead.
Football games, bonfires and camping, hot
cocoa, s'mores and napping. Cuddling under the
starry sky, having no worries as time passes by.
That time of year to harvest and reap, when we
all get together to give thanks and eat.
The beautiful colors, the cool, crisp air, are some
wonderful things we'll find there.
Saleta Anne Gray

I Thought We Were Friends

I Thought We Were Friends

What defines a person as a friend? One to whom you can confide in. One who picks you up when your down. One that's always there no matter what's going down. A person you love and admire just because they are themselves.
What draws us to these strangers and makes us feel like we couldn't make it without them???
Perhaps the power of all life, the one who gave us our life. God.
Does He give us friends for seasons, does He give us friends for reasons. Questions I'm sure to ask when I finally get to meet Him.
So you say, "I thought we were friends," as if I actually mattered to you. My loyalty, my words, and my heart was all yours. You couldn't accept my words as truth...so "I thought we were friends," means what, exactly to you.
Saleta Anne Gray

I Am Beautiful

I Am Beautiful

I am beautiful both inside and out.
Created by God, put here on this earth to love
and to learn what life's all about.
Beautifully flawed, masterfully created to share
truth and joy to everyone around.
Truly blessed, much more than I deserve,
eternally great full for the lessons I've learned.
Scars on my body, my mind, and my soul, each
one placed there for the master to mold.
Blessings and lessons disguised as friends,
lovers, and foes, never knowing what each one
foretold.
Spirituality grounded, saved by Grace, I can't
wait to look upon the master's glorious face.
Words and wisdom learned from others who
were placed here to help make me find the true
meaning of this woman I am.
Beautiful imperfection is all I'll ever be, created
by God to teach us all that this journey is about
much more than just me…
Saleta Anne Gray

9 Years Today

9 Years Today

Nine years have come and gone.
Seasons have changed and birds have flown, but
missing you is never gone.

I heard your favorite song yesterday, and tears
just streamed down my face. It wasn't the lyrics
or even the tune, it was just the thought of me
missing you.

They say it gets easier as time goes by, but now I
know, that's one big lie. There's nothing easy
when your memory comes around, because I
know that you're no longer around.

No one to turn to since you went away, because
friends like you aren't born everyday.

I've seen you in my dreams from time to time,
and I feel like you're still here by my side. Then
when I wake up reality sets in, I'm still missing
my very best friend.

Your memory remains deep in my heart, even though it's been torn all apart.

Year after year, I still think of you and all of the things we used to do.

There are lots things I still want to share, but at they end of the day, you're still not there.

There's one thing that I know, as long as I'm living, I'll never let your memory go, because the memories we shared mean more now to me than ever before.

All my love, Saleta ♥♥♥

When I No Longer Remember Your Names

When I No Longer Remember Your Names

As I grow older and my memory starts to fade,
and I no longer remember your names…please
be patient with me and remember the times I
called you by name.
Always remember that no matter what, I have
loved you all and have known you one by one.
From the day you were born, until the day I die,
I will carry the love between you and I.
So when that moment comes and I can't
remember your name, just know from now until
then, you've been forever etched into the heart
of this one.
I may have been your wife, your daughter, or
your son, whenever it happens, remember I'm
not the only one. Others have suffered the same
disease as me, just always remember to be
patient with me.
Keep loving me as much as you always have,
and remind yourself that my love for you will
forever last.
Saleta Gray

What If…

What If…

What if we all focused on spreading love instead of hate…
What if we all decided to come together as one…
What if we stop focusing on all of the negativity and focus on each other…
What if we were completely honest with ourselves and not what others think…
What if we changed the world with love for our fellow man…
Just imagine if all of the "what if's" in our lives actually happened…
That's the world I want to live in…
What if you change the way you see yourself and the world around you…
What if you just focused on everything this world has to offer…
This life is about love and peace…make a decision to choose just that everyday…
Watch how incredible your life will be by changing the way you treat yourself…
If you can love yourself first, then loving the rest of the world will be easy…

Make peace within and you will be able to share it with the rest of the world…
What if you turn off the noise around you, would you then be able to ask the tough questions and then seek and find the answers…
What if…
Saleta Gray

Mother's Day Without You

Mother's Day Without You

Another year has passed and Mother's Day is here. A time for love and laughter that has been shared through out the years. My heart is very heavy and my eyes they fill with tears, not because you are in Heaven, but because you are no longer here, to share today and those to come with happiness and cheers. I will cherish the memories of the time we shared here, until the day God calls my name and with you I shall remain. Happy Heavenly Mother's Day mama, I love and miss you more than you will ever know.
All my love, Leta 🤍🤍🤍

19 Years

Happy Birthday Alex 🤍🤍🤍 19 years have come and gone so very quickly!!!

19 years of joy and tears. A Christmas blessing I will cherish for years. A bundle of love from God above. A bouncing baby boy with eyes so blue, and a heart full of love so true. I couldn't imagine not having you here, you bring me joy year after year. A handsome young man you have grown into, always smiling with your eyes of blue. Words cannot measure the pride in my heart. You will never know how much you are loved and how much I prayed for you to God up above. As I sit back and watch you grow into a man, I pray I have done everything in God's plan. All of my life I could never imagine a greater gift than the one sent from Heaven, the one God chose to call me mama and bring me happiness again and again.

May you always remember I prayed for you son and God gave me my answer in the form of you son.

I love you and I pray that God will continue to bless you today and always 🤍🤍🤍🤍 love forever, mama 🥰🥰🥰🥰

Life Through A Windshield

Life Through A Windshield

You never even notice that I can see you over there. Out in the yard, working on your car. Out in the street riding your bike or playing basketball with your peeps. I never stopped, just kept driving by. Watching as I passed you in the driver's seat, talking on your phone, singing out loud, or doing other things that shouldn't be allowed…Every little town, rolling into the big cities, you'd never even know I was paying attention. A blessing and a curse watching what you do, longing for the day that I'll be home too. Life through the windshield can be peaceful at times, when driving through the mountains for a moment in time, I seem to get lost somewhere in my mind, not thinking about home or the loved ones I've left behind. Then in a flash my reality kicks in, I'm still on this old road missing my family and friends. A way of life that many can't understand, but it's the way we chose to make a living my friend. Glorious scenery from God up above mixed with emotions of sadness and love. A lot of time to reflect on the life I have lived, sometimes it's hard to swallow this pill. But we

keep driving on over the next hill, because every
mile traveled keeps paying the bills. It won't be
long now, I can see home by morning light, just
remember I was watching, longing for your life.
Saleta A. Gray

My Angel, My Friend

"My Angel, My Friend"
There will never be another friend like you,
someone who knows me through and through.
From the day we met and throughout the years,
we have shared our sorrows and tears, our
laughter and fears. No matter what time day or
night you were always there when I needed
advise. You are never one to ask for help, you
always try to do everything yourself. I have
never known anyone like you, you face this
world with no fear it seems. You are a shining
light that always beams. A loving mother to Von,
Shaun, and Tia. A beautiful woman both inside
and out. A friend like no other, their rock and
loving mother. What did I do to deserve a friend
like you? I don't have a clue, but I thank God for
leading me to you!! There are no words that will
ever describe the love for you I feel inside. God
sends Angels to walk among us. I know this is
true because he sent us you!!! All my love
forever, Saleta

Missing You

Missing You

Missing you is nothing new, I do it every day.
Ever since you left, my heart feels it every day.
Sometimes a song, sometimes a scent, a spoken
word, or a letter that you sent; brings back
memories I never will forget.
A picture of you, I have a few, that reminds me
every day of my one dear friend I would love to
see again.
A song that plays reminds me of days when we
lived carefree; never dreaming at that moment
one of our lives would end.
Oh the many times I've laid here and I've cried
wishing I could change how our story ends.
So many times I wished deep down inside I
could take away your pain. You were always so
strong and now that your gone I feel myself
slipping away.
No one will ever understand what you meant to
me and never again will I have another friend
that could ever take your place!!
All my love forever, Saleta
In loving memory of my very best friend, Judy
Marie Mitchell.

Happy Heavenly Birthday Mama

Happy Heavenly Birthday Mama

Happy Heavenly Birthday Mama,
Today you're not alone, I know that you're with
God today in your Heavenly home.
There will always be an emptiness I carry within
my soul, for the day God called you away I
wasn't ready to let you go.
They say you're in a better place and now you
know no pain, I believe that's true but since the
day I lost you, I haven't been the same.
They tell me time heals everything but I don't
know if that is true, because today I feel the
same pain in my heart for you.
Today we celebrate the life you lived and though
it's not the same, here in my heart is a place for
you that always will remain.
Happy Heavenly Birthday Mama, until we meet
again.
Your loving daughter, Saleta

Mama

Mama

For 48 years I have had you with me. I don't know how to say goodbye. I'm always the one to be strong and do whatever you need from dusk till dawn. You were always just a phone call away and I always knew it every day. Now I'm lost knowing you will be gone sitting and waiting for the ringing of my phone. 48 years I was blessed to have you so near and now I'm just in a state of fear. No words can say what you mean to me and I'll be lost while you are at peace. No more suffering and no more pain God will restore your health once again. Heaven will gain a beautiful soul and I will be left with an empty hole. God has your name in the book of life and now there will be no suffering and strife. I know one day I'll see you again, but until then I've lost my very best friend. I love you more than words can say and I can't wait for you to meet me at Heaven's gate on that glorious day.

Saleta Gray

I Didn't Forget Your Birthday

Judy Marie Mitchell

I didn't forget your birthday, I just didn't know what to say.

My heart's been filled with sadness since the day you went away.

I know it was God's will, but I still can't help but feel like a part of me has died without you by my side.

Your birthday will always be an extra special day to me, because April 30th is the day God created the best friend that will ever be.

So happy birthday once again in Heaven my dear sweet friend. I know one day I will see you again but I know I will miss you every day until then. All my love, Saleta 🩶

Hornet Pride

What is "HORNET PRIDE?" you say.
It's something we live day by day.
You can see it on signs up and down our streets.
You can see it on the clothes we wear, you can
see it almost everywhere.
Football, Baseball, Archery, or Tennis, Golf,
Track, Basketball, Softball and Soccer of course.
No matter what season or sport you choose,
HORNET PRIDE we'll never lose!! You can
hear it when our Hornets pull up, throughout the
game, and even on our bus. People lined up and
down Main Street just to catch a peek at our
players who can't be beat!!! Our stands are
packed, no room in the back, as proud Hornet
fans shout as loudly as they can. Pride for each
individual player, and as a team we pray
together. The boy's of fall seem to start it all.
Their Friday night lights seem to ignite our
Hornet Pride each and every time. Hornet Pride
you see, is something that brings our tiny town
together and no matter where we go, you can bet
that other folks know, in our eyes, there is

nothing stronger than our HORNET PRIDE!!!!
🐝 🤍 🤍 🤍 🤍 🤍 🤍 🐝

Saleta Gray

Like Father, Like Son

Like Father, Like Son

 A relationship like no other,
The bond of a farther and a son.
It all began day you were born, my life as a
father and you as my son.
So many things to teach and show you, so many
memories we create day by day.
From riding your bike to driving a truck, a few
years later racing with each other and pressing
our luck. So many memories we have made
along the way, from learning to walk and to
loving each other, making mistakes and
struggling at times, never giving up on our faith
in each other. From lessons learned and advice
we've been given, creating a bond that will
never be forgotten. God has blessed us along the
way, and on His promises we shall stand. When
times are hard always remember I love you and I
know you love me, our father-son bond will
always be. Nothing in this world could ever
break it, thank God each day He let us make it.

Saleta Gray
May 28,2018

Still Missing You

Still Missing You Judy

Two years have come and gone, and time has continued to move on. The emptiness that lasts can't undo the past, the moments you were here until your very last. The memories we share are almost more than I can bare, and then sometimes they are the last things on my mind. It still seems unreal, like my life is standing still. My one and only true best friend will never be here again. Instead, she's gone away, to live among Angels everyday. In my heart you will remain, until God calls my name.
All my love, Saleta 🩶

I Hit My Knees And Pray

25

Just when it seems like all hope is gone, I remember to hit my knees and pray. To pray for God's will and to help me make it another day. I pray for understanding and the strength to go on. On His promise I stand accepting whatever is in His plan. Not questioning why, what, or how, just knowing that whatever His plan is, it's better than my own. Thank you God for the comfort you bring and the peace you give, allowing me to be able to live.
Amen.
Saleta Gray

www.ingramcontent.com/pod-product-compliance
Lightning Source LLC
La Vergne TN
LVHW051246200726
843510LV00011B/1707